MW00479714

God's

Little Book™

of Big Bible Promises

GOD'S little book OF BIG Bible promises

KATHERINE J. BUTLER

GENERAL EDITOR

TYNDALE HOUSE PUBLISHERS

CAROL STREAM, ILLINOIS

LIVING EXPRESSIONS COLLECTION

Living Expressions invites you to explore God's Word in a way that is refreshing to the spirit and restorative to the soul.

Visit Tyndale online at tyndale.com.

TYNDALE, Tyndale's quill logo, *Living Expressions*, and the Living Expressions logo are registered trademarks of Tyndale House Ministries. *God's Little Book* is a trademark of Tyndale House Ministries.

God's Little Book of Big Bible Promises

Copyright © 2021 by Ronald A. Beers. All rights reserved.

Adapted from *365 Pocket Promises from the Bible* (ISBN 978-1-4143-6986-0), copyright © 2012 by Ronald A. Beers.

General editor: Katherine J. Butler

Contributing editors: Ronald A. Beers and Amy E. Mason

Cover photograph of fabric texture copyright © SPIN/Adobe Stock. All rights reserved.

Cover illustrations of hand-drawn decorations copyright © Julia Henze/Shutterstock. All rights reserved.

Cover illustration of seamless pattern copyright © Oleksandra/Adobe Stock. All rights reserved.

Interior illustration of floral ornament copyright © More Images/Adobe Stock. All rights reserved.

Interior illustration of floral borders copyright © Bariskina/Shutterstock. All rights reserved.

Interior illustration of floral vine copyright © iStockphoto. All rights reserved.

Designed by Nicole Grimes

Scripture quotations are taken from the *Holy Bible*, New Living Translation, copyright © 1996, 2004, 2015 by Tyndale House Foundation. Used by permission of Tyndale House Publishers, Carol Stream, Illinois 60188. All rights reserved.

For information about special discounts for bulk purchases, please contact Tyndale House Publishers at csresponse@tyndale.com, or call 1-800-323-9400.

ISBN 978-1-4964-4644-2

Printed in China

27   26   25   24   23   22   21
7   6   5   4   3   2   1

TABLE OF CONTENTS

ANXIETY. FEAR. HELPLESSNESS. Despair. Discontentment. Jealousy. Impatience. These kinds of feelings rule over our hearts when we fail to believe God's promises for us in his Word. God's promises bring stability and security to chaos. They cultivate comfort and hope during times of bleakness and inspire freedom and joy when we are desolate.

Perhaps you struggle to know where and how to search the Bible to find God's promises. This little book is the perfect place to start. We have carefully selected 150 promises from the Bible and have organized them by topic to help you find the right promise for your particular situation or need.

But before you begin, keep this in mind: Resist the temptation to skim God's Word. Do not let it slip away from your mind as quickly as it came in. Every time you read a promise, read it again and again and let the truth of it sink in. Ask yourself, *Do I believe this?* And sit in the truth that each promise is made to you personally by your Creator.

God has promised big things for you in this life and the life to come. Our hope and prayer is that these promises will stick with you, positively impacting the way you think and live.

Abandonment

Those who know your name trust in you, for you, O LORD, do not abandon those who search for you.

PSALM 9:10

There may be times when even those closest to you neglect or abandon you, but know that God never will. He promises his unfailing love to those who search for him. The moments you feel deserted and alone may just be the times you need to look more intently and see that God is there by your side. He is always trying to get your attention. Are you aware of him? If you are sincerely seeking him, then you are sure to find him.

Abiding in Christ

[Jesus said,] "Remain in me, and I will remain in you. For a branch cannot produce fruit if it is severed from the vine, and you cannot be fruitful unless you remain in me. Yes, I am the vine; you are the branches. Those who remain in me, and I in them, will produce much fruit. For apart from me you can do nothing."

JOHN 15:4-5

When you are connected to Jesus, he can turn your simple acts of service into profound and purposeful moments. God uses even the smallest acts—simple words of encouragement, humble gifts, and seemingly insignificant moments in which you share your testimony—to produce big results. Stay connected to Jesus and abide in his ways. Let him turn your every act and word into wonderful works for the Kingdom of God.

Addiction

The Holy Spirit produces this kind of fruit in our lives: love, joy, peace, patience, kindness, goodness, faithfulness, gentleness, and self-control.

GALATIANS 5:22-23

We all have our addictions, whether they are simply bad habits or serious dependencies. But one thing we are all dangerously addicted to is sin. We consistently—daily—disobey God's Word through sinful thoughts, words, and actions. The only cure is to submit to the control of God through his Holy Spirit. When you are under God's control, the Holy Spirit replaces what's destructive in your life with what's beneficial. God's transforming power is the only thing that can ultimately heal you from your addictions.

Adversity

God is our refuge and strength, always ready to help in times of trouble.

PSALM 46:1

One thing you can count on in your lifetime is that adversity will come. The question is, What will you do when it arrives? When you believe in Jesus, Satan will work overtime to send you trials and temptations, hoping these difficult situations will make you doubt God and stop seeking him. But don't despair. Adversity may be a sign that you are being faithful to God. So continue to be faithful, even when things get tough. God promises to strengthen you through these troubling times and protect you through any harm.

Aging

I will be your God throughout your lifetime—
until your hair is white with age. I made you,
and I will care for you.

ISAIAH 46:4

Many people associate aging with weight
gain, wrinkles, and gray hair. But what if we as
believers viewed aging differently? What if we
saw each passing year as an opportunity to
experience more of God's tender care for us?
God promises to walk with us throughout our
lifetime, to watch over us in each and every
stage. Reflect on how God has blessed you over
the years, and ask him to use these memories
to deepen your faith and trust in him.

Anxiety

Give all your worries and cares to God,
for he cares about you.

1 PETER 5:7

How does God care for you? Can you count the ways? If you struggle with anxious thoughts and worries, remember that God promises he is always close, ready to help in your time of need. His presence surrounds you and protects you from Satan's attacks. He sends you opportunities and blessings to make your life full and satisfying. He promises to take your worries and cares upon himself. The next time you experience fearful thoughts, draw close to the Lord. Tell him your every worry because he promises to care for you.

Approaching God

Come close to God, and God will come close to you.

JAMES 4:8

Our natural human tendency is to cover our sin or hide from God when we have done something wrong. A clear example of this in Scripture is the story of Adam and Eve. After they disobeyed God by eating from the tree of the knowledge of good and evil, they covered their nakedness and hid from God. But God promises you can always enter his presence with confidence. There is no need to run away from the God who longs to be close to you. Step out of hiding and experience the peace, love, and joy that can come only when you are in close relationship with him.

Approval

The master said, "Well done, my good and faithful servant. You have been faithful in handling this small amount, so now I will give you many more responsibilities. Let's celebrate together!"

MATTHEW 25:23

Those who consistently do a good job in their workplace or profession are usually trusted with more freedom and responsibility. Their work receives praise and approval from their supervisor. In the same way, the more you serve God faithfully, the more he will reward you and give you opportunities to serve him. Remember that you don't have to earn God's love, but he desires for you to serve him well with the gifts he's given you.

Assurance

If we are faithful to the end, trusting God just as firmly as when we first believed, we will share in all that belongs to Christ.

HEBREWS 3:14

The moment you believe that Jesus died on the cross to save you and then confess your sins to him, acknowledging that he is Lord of all, you are saved from God's judgment and given eternal life. You can be sure of this through God's promises in Scripture. As your life progresses, always seek to have an active, growing friendship with Jesus. This will help assure you that you will enjoy eternal life with him and share in his Kingdom.

Attitude

Be strong and immovable. Always work enthusiastically for the Lord, for you know that nothing you do for the Lord is ever useless.

1 CORINTHIANS 15:58

Attitude is important because it affects your thoughts, motives, and actions. As a believer in Christ, you can maintain a positive attitude through hardships and adversity. You can know that the God of the universe created you, loves you, and promises you salvation and eternal life, where pain and disappointment are no more. God is working for you, not against you. Remind yourself of these truths every day. They will positively affect your attitude, which will in turn enhance the way you live and serve God.

Balance

Letting your sinful nature control your mind leads to death. But letting the Spirit control your mind leads to life and peace.

ROMANS 8:6

Establishing balance in your life means using your gifts, time, and resources to honor God. It also means caring for others and yourself. This practice begins with allowing God to speak to you about what in your life is truly important, to assure you there is time for everything he calls you to do. Jesus, despite his power and the needs of those around him, still took time to rest, pray, and celebrate with friends while working toward what God had planned for him to do. When you try to accomplish too much, you usually fall short and feel unsatisfied. But when you let the Holy Spirit guide your mind and desires, the balance he brings gives you peace of heart and mind.

Becoming like Christ

All of us who have had that veil removed can see and reflect the glory of the Lord. And the Lord—who is the Spirit—makes us more and more like him as we are changed into his glorious image.

2 CORINTHIANS 3:18

The more time two people spend together, the more alike they usually become. Each person adopts certain figures of speech or attributes of the other, even to the point of sometimes dressing or thinking alike. The same is true when you spend time with Jesus. As you grow in relationship with him, your speech becomes more gentle and kind, your face mirrors his joy, your attitudes and motives become more pure, and your actions become more focused on serving others. After all, when Christ changes you, it's always for the better!

Belief

God saved you by his grace when you believed. And you can't take credit for this; it is a gift from God.

EPHESIANS 2:8

Remember that it is through grace alone that God has saved you. He approves of you not because of what you have or have not done, but because he loves you and has forgiven all your sins. The fact that this is God's free gift to you and not something you must strive for with your own effort brings great comfort, security, and hope. When you accept God's grace just as you would accept any other gift, you will fully enjoy its benefits.

Blamelessness

[God] has reconciled you to himself through the death of Christ in his physical body. As a result, he has brought you into his own presence, and you are holy and blameless as you stand before him without a single fault.

COLOSSIANS 1:22

Being holy and blameless before God doesn't mean you no longer sin. Instead it means you grow in holiness by wholly dedicating and devoting yourself to God, becoming distinct and separate from the world's way of living as you remain committed to godly living and purity. When you put your faith in Christ, God makes you holy by forgiving your sins. When he looks at you, he sees the righteousness of Jesus and declares you blameless, as if you had never sinned. Apart from him, you could never live a life of perfect holiness. But as his follower, you can choose each day to be more like him.

Boldness

Because of Christ and our faith in him, we can now come boldly and confidently into God's presence.

EPHESIANS 3:12

Boldness comes from confidence in God's promise that those who trust in Jesus as their Savior can come boldly into his presence without fear. Jesus' work on the cross means that all who follow him are fully forgiven and fully accepted in his sight. Allow your confidence in this truth to shape you to live each day with boldness.

Brokenness

The sacrifice you desire is a broken spirit. You will not reject a broken and repentant heart, O God.

PSALM 51:17

Sometimes brokenness is a consequence of personal sin or someone else's sin against you. Regardless of how your brokenness came to be, God promises to be close to those whose spirits are broken. Repenting of your sin means turning to God for forgiveness so he can begin to heal and restore you. He also promises to use your brokenness for good. Ask God to help you recognize your need for him and assure you of his presence in your pain.

Capability

The LORD asked Moses, "Who makes a person's mouth? Who decides whether people speak or do not speak, hear or do not hear, see or do not see? Is it not I, the LORD? Now go! I will be with you as you speak, and I will instruct you in what to say."

EXODUS 4:11-12

When God asks you to do something, he gives you the abilities and resources you need to get the job done. Moses didn't think he had the power of persuasion to confront Pharaoh on behalf of God's people, but God promised to be with him and to give him the right words to say. Even when you think you cannot accomplish the task God has put before you, remember that he is with you and will give you what you need to carry out his will.

Celebration

[Jesus said,] "In the same way, there is joy in the presence of God's angels when even one sinner repents."

LUKE 15:10

Heaven is filled with celebrations too wonderful for the human mind to imagine. Angels worship God in mighty celebration and rejoice wildly when just one sinner repents. One day all believers will celebrate together at the great banquet of the Lord in heaven. As a follower of Jesus, you can look forward with great anticipation to that day when you, too, will be able to join in these heavenly events.

Comfort

All praise to God, the Father of our Lord Jesus Christ. God is our merciful Father and the source of all comfort. He comforts us in all our troubles so that we can comfort others. When they are troubled, we will be able to give them the same comfort God has given us.

2 CORINTHIANS 1:3-4

Think of all the ways God has comforted you in times of trouble. When you have experienced his assuring love, guiding wisdom, and sustaining power, you desire to model that kind of comfort to others. You see their need and better understand how to be a source of peace and light to them. You want to show them God's comfort so they may in turn take what they've been given and comfort others as well.

Commitment

Love the Lord your God and . . . keep his commands, decrees, and regulations by walking in his ways. If you do this, you will live . . . and the Lord your God will bless you.

DEUTERONOMY 30:16

Serving God with your entire life begins with serving him in smaller, simpler ways. Commit the little, daily choices to him. The more you do so, the more you will obey him in all things. Obedience is the result of a lifelong commitment to make godly choices on a daily basis.

Community

[Jesus said,] "Where two or three gather together as my followers, I am there among them."

MATTHEW 18:20

God lives in the heart of every believer, but he also lives within the community of the church. When the church is gathered together, God meets his people in a special way. Just as being present with other fans at a live concert or sports event makes it much more exciting, participating with other believers in worshiping God makes the experience much more meaningful.

Compassion

He will rescue the poor when they cry to him;
he will help the oppressed, who have no one to
defend them. He feels pity for the weak and the
needy . . . for their lives are precious to him.

PSALM 72:12-14

Our world is full of people who are desperate
to experience the compassion of Jesus in their
lives. Compassion is about opening our hearts
to those around us who are hurting. It involves
caring for the people Jesus cared for—the poor,
oppressed, and weak. Ask God to open your
eyes to those around you who need his love
and kindness. Let him pierce your heart with
compassion so you can be his hands and feet
to this hurting world.

Confession

If we confess our sins to him, he is faithful and just to forgive us our sins and to cleanse us from all wickedness.

1 JOHN 1:9

Confession acknowledges the sin within your heart. When you realize the ugliness of your sin, it can feel embarrassing and painful. After all, it's never easy to look deep into the dark places of your life, to become vulnerable and open yourself to rebuke. But confession is a necessary part of knowing God, receiving forgiveness and freedom from sin, and identifying yourself as a follower of Jesus Christ. God's supply of forgiveness far exceeds what your sins demand. No matter how many sins you confess or how often you confess them, God promises to forgive you whenever you ask.

Confidence

Those who are righteous will be long remembered. They do not fear bad news; they confidently trust the Lord to care for them. They are confident and fearless and can face their foes triumphantly.

PSALM 112:6-8

We are confident in someone when we recognize complete consistency between their words, actions, and outcomes. You can be completely confident in what God says in his Word because he has never broken a single promise. God has always done what he said he would do, and he will always be trustworthy in your circumstances.

Contentment

By his divine power, God has given us everything we need for living a godly life. We have received all of this by coming to know him, the one who called us to himself by means of his marvelous glory and excellence.

2 PETER 1:3

When your contentment depends on things going your way, you will face disappointment when they don't. When your contentment comes from watching Jesus meet your needs, you will be secure and happy knowing that God is working out his plan for you, which is always best. And as you grow in relationship with him, he will help you to discern what is valuable in life and what is distracting.

Coping

The LORD helps the fallen and lifts those bent beneath their loads.

PSALM 145:14

Life is stressful. New challenges and pressures often come your way, and painful seasons of life are inevitable. It can be easy to wonder how to cope with it all. While you can't always control your circumstances, you can control how you respond to them and whom you go to for help. God encourages you to work through your problems instead of running away from them. By turning to him for help, you will come out stronger on the other side. He offers strength and wisdom to help you respond well to life's setbacks and hurts, and he gives you grace and comfort by carrying your burdens for you.

Courage

*Don't be afraid, for I am with you. Don't be
discouraged, for I am your God. I will strengthen
you and help you. I will hold you up with my
victorious right hand.*

ISAIAH 41:10

To experience fear is normal, but to be
paralyzed by fear can be an indication that you
doubt God's promises or his ability to care for
you in the face of danger. Realize that courage
doesn't come from your qualifications or your
credentials but from the promise of God's
presence and power. When you know God is
with you and helping you, you can face any
fear.

Culture

Don't copy the behavior and customs of this world, but let God transform you into a new person by changing the way you think. Then you will learn to know God's will for you, which is good and pleasing and perfect.

ROMANS 12:2

God's message has always been countercultural. He calls believers to follow a path that looks different from the ways of the world. When we decide to stand against certain worldviews, pray for our enemies, or give extravagantly, our actions may not make sense to our neighbors, but it's important we do so anyway. Rather than allowing your culture to influence you, choose to reflect on God's Word, and ask God to help you influence the culture around you.

Death

Our dying bodies must be transformed into bodies that will never die; our mortal bodies must be transformed into immortal bodies. Then . . . this Scripture will be fulfilled: "Death is swallowed up in victory. O death, where is your victory? O death, where is your sting?"

1 CORINTHIANS 15:53-55

So often we see death as terrible, but what an adventure awaits those who love Jesus! When Christians die, they go on to meet God in heaven. Their earthly bodies will eventually be transformed into bodies that will never again be subject to sin, pain, death, and the limitations of this world, and they will live with God forever. What could be better than this wonderful gift?

Defender

The angel of the LORD is a guard; he surrounds and defends all who fear him.

PSALM 34:7

The God who has already defeated evil is always with you. Because you are his child, you can be sure he will deliver you from evil too. Sometimes God may step into a situation to rescue you by using other people, while other times he may send supernatural help through angels—his warriors who are in constant battle against Satan and the powers of evil. No matter how God chooses to work, be assured of his presence with you and his promise to defend you.

Deliverance

[Jesus said,] "The Spirit of the LORD is upon me, for he has anointed me to bring Good News to the poor. He has sent me to proclaim that captives will be released, that the blind will see, that the oppressed will be set free, and that the time of the LORD's favor has come."

LUKE 4:18-19

Jesus came to deliver people oppressed by the world and the powers of evil. We see numerous examples of this throughout the Gospels. Jesus delivered people from spiritual oppression by driving out demons, from physical oppression by healing their diseases, and from intellectual oppression by exposing lies and teaching the truth that set them free. Jesus not only promises to deliver you but also promises to protect you from the forces that oppress you in this world.

Desires

God is working in you, giving you the desire and the power to do what pleases him.

PHILIPPIANS 2:13

God doesn't force change on you. When you invite him into your life as your personal Savior, you give him permission to use his power to change you. Trying to change on your own will only leave you discouraged, but letting God do the work of transformation in you will last a lifetime. You will see dramatic changes in your attitudes and actions when you allow God to do the work only he can do.

Dignity

You made [human beings] only a little lower than God and crowned them with glory and honor.

PSALM 8:5

To have dignity means to understand who God made you to be—a human being who bears his image. In the eyes of the Creator, you have great worth and value, and you have been made for a special purpose. Your dignity comes not from what others think about you but from God himself, who chose to create you and give you unique gifts and abilities. This truth not only reassures you of your dignity but also gives you the confidence to boldly serve him wherever he leads you.

Discernment

Let those who are wise understand these things.
Let those with discernment listen carefully.
The paths of the LORD are true and right, and
righteous people live by walking in them. But
in those paths sinners stumble and fall.

HOSEA 14:9

Discernment is the ability to distinguish between right and wrong by training and disciplining your conscience, mind, senses, and body. The Bible says that discernment is necessary for you to mature in your faith. When you develop discernment, you are able to recognize and resist temptation before it can engulf you. You learn the difference between truth and lies, between God's voice and the voices of sin and Satan. When you practice discernment, you avoid the pitfalls and confusion that temptation and sin cause. You walk in God's ways, which lead you to a more fulfilling life.

Discipline

No discipline is enjoyable while it is happening—it's painful! But afterward there will be a peaceful harvest of right living for those who are trained in this way.

HEBREWS 12:11

The goal of discipline is to prevent you from harming yourself and others. Sin always hurts your relationship with God and others, but God's discipline is an act of love to keep you from damaging those relationships. Left to yourself, you may move away from God and toward sin. But his discipline reminds you of the right way to live and helps you become the person he created you to be. God promises that the ultimate result of his discipline is blessing.

Discouragement

Be strong and courageous! Do not be afraid or discouraged. For the LORD your God is with you wherever you go.

JOSHUA 1:9

Discouragement is never from God. Instead, God uses his power to help you understand that he is stronger than your biggest problem or fiercest enemy. While fear and discouragement come from feeling alone against a great threat, courage comes from knowing that God is beside you, helping you to fight that threat. Be encouraged by focusing more on God's presence surrounding you and less on the problem at hand.

Endurance

Dear brothers and sisters, when troubles of any kind come your way, consider it an opportunity for great joy. For you know that when your faith is tested, your endurance has a chance to grow. So let it grow, for when your endurance is fully developed, you will be perfect and complete, needing nothing.

JAMES 1:2-4

It may seem contradictory, but adversity actually produces strength. Just as your muscles grow when they are pushed beyond their limits, your character grows when the pressures of life test your strength and endurance. Developing strong character takes time and attention. Only through hard work will you achieve great accomplishments and the satisfaction that goes with them. Pain, trials, and temptations refine us so that over time we are better equipped to endure them.

Enemies

If God is for us, who can ever be against us?

ROMANS 8:31

The powers of evil can seem overwhelming at times. In those moments of struggle, you may be afraid and wonder how you will keep going. But God promises he will be your shield. When you are afraid, the courage you need comes only from realizing how powerful God is. No enemy can stand before him. God is more powerful than any force that comes against you.

Eternity

This world is not our permanent home; we are looking forward to a home yet to come.

HEBREWS 13:14

As a heaven-bound follower of Jesus, try to put your earthly and heavenly lives in perspective. On earth, you will likely live fewer than a hundred years. In heaven, one hundred million years will be just the beginning. In light of this truth, you should spend your time on earth preparing yourself for heaven. Having an eternal perspective today will help you live with the right priorities and prepare you for spending eternity with God.

Faith

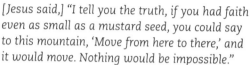

[Jesus said,] "I tell you the truth, if you had faith even as small as a mustard seed, you could say to this mountain, 'Move from here to there,' and it would move. Nothing would be impossible."

MATTHEW 17:20

In biblical times, the mustard seed was known as one of the smallest seeds, so it was often used to illustrate something of the tiniest size. Using this example in one of his parables, Jesus taught that it is not the size of your faith that makes the difference but the size of the one in whom you put your faith. To see and experience all that God can do, you don't need to have great faith in him; rather, you must only have faith that he is a great God.

Faithfulness

If we are unfaithful, he remains faithful, for he cannot deny who he is.

2 TIMOTHY 2:13

Do you love others genuinely? Are you faithful to your family and friends? Faithfulness is important for maintaining loving relationships, because even those closest to you will disappoint you at times, just as you have disappointed God. But despite your unfaithfulness, God loves you and remains faithful to you. Model that same love to others, and remain faithful to them even when they fail you. Your steadfastness will show that your love is genuine.

Fear

The LORD is my light and my salvation—so why should I be afraid? The LORD is my fortress, protecting me from danger, so why should I tremble?

PSALM 27:1

Fear turns your focus away from God and toward the troubles that intimidate you. Look at your fears as opportunities to rely on God for his help, guidance, and saving power. No problem is too big for the God who promises to save you and be with you in the midst of harm.

Following Jesus

At the name of Jesus every knee should bow, in heaven and on earth and under the earth, and every tongue declare that Jesus Christ is Lord, to the glory of God the Father.

PHILIPPIANS 2:10-11

People have all kinds of excuses for avoiding Jesus—they're too busy, they see him as the cause of their hardships, they procrastinate, they don't want to give up their favorite vices, or maybe they just don't know where to begin. But the Bible promises that the day will come when we all must face Jesus, and he will know whether we have declared him Lord of our lives. Today, God is inviting you to deal with any excuses you may have so you will be prepared for when that day arrives.

Forgiveness

Though your sins are like scarlet, I will make them as white as snow. Though they are red like crimson, I will make them as white as wool.

ISAIAH 1:18

God's forgiveness means that he looks at you as though you had never sinned. It means that you stand blameless before him. When God forgives you, he doesn't sweep your sins under the carpet; he promises to completely wash them away and make you as pure and perfect as his Son, Jesus.

Friendship with God

Since our friendship with God was restored by the death of his Son while we were still his enemies, we will certainly be saved through the life of his Son. So now we can rejoice in our wonderful new relationship with God because our Lord Jesus Christ has made us friends of God.

ROMANS 5:10-11

The God of the universe desires friendship with us. We simply must want it, too, but unfortunately, many of us don't. True friends hold each other accountable and do whatever they can to please each other. Yet many people don't want the kind of life that pleases God. They don't realize that pleasing him gives life true meaning and joy. God created us to be in relationships, especially in a relationship with him through faith in Jesus Christ. As you develop your relationship with God, you develop a friendship with him. He is your Lord, but he also calls you friend. Lean into that friendship today.

Future

We know that God causes everything to work together for the good of those who love God and are called according to his purpose for them.

ROMANS 8:28

When you believe that Jesus died on the cross to spare you from eternal punishment and give you the gift of everlasting life, then the troubles of this world no longer seem as threatening. You know that your future—for all eternity—is secure. This assurance will give you peace no matter what happens in your lifetime, and it will change the way you react to the troubles and trials that may come your way.

Gifts

This is how God loved the world: He gave his one and only Son, so that everyone who believes in him will not perish but have eternal life.

JOHN 3:16

The greatest gift God offers you is his Son, Jesus. Through Jesus, God gives you the gift of eternal life as well as his abiding presence in your life today. What makes these gifts so wonderful is that you don't have to earn them. Instead you simply must accept them by believing in Jesus as your Savior. Take comfort in knowing that nothing—and no one—can take them away.

Giving

[Jesus said,] "Give, and you will receive. Your gift will return to you in full—pressed down, shaken together to make room for more, running over, and poured into your lap. The amount you give will determine the amount you get back."

LUKE 6:38

The act of giving creates a cycle of blessing. As God gives abundantly to you, you can give abundantly back to him and others through your time, talents, and financial gifts. This, in turn, can lead others to give abundantly to God as well. God promises that when you give, you will receive blessing in return.

Goals

Sympathize with each other. Love each other as brothers and sisters. Be tenderhearted, and keep a humble attitude. Don't repay evil for evil. Don't retaliate with insults when people insult you. Instead, pay them back with a blessing. That is what God has called you to do, and he will grant you his blessing.

1 PETER 3:8-9

While it's good to set larger goals for your family, career, and personal achievements, it's also important to set smaller daily goals for your spiritual life. You can determine today to be kind toward others, to be humble, to respond gracefully if someone takes advantage of you, to read your Bible, and to share an encouraging word. These small goals will bring great rewards when practiced over a lifetime. God promises to bless your obedience to him through these faithful actions. They become the essential building blocks of all that God wants you to accomplish.

Godly Living

Commit everything you do to the LORD.
Trust him, and he will help you.

PSALM 37:5

Being committed to God means trusting him
to lead you and do what is best for you. It also
means resolving to do your best to obey his
Word in all areas of your life. Begin each day by
committing to follow God while remembering
that he has already committed to lead you.

God's Care

Give your burdens to the LORD, and he will take care of you. He will not permit the godly to slip and fall.

PSALM 55:22

God cares for you and helps you whenever you ask. When you bring your burdens to him in prayer, you experience freedom from worry and anxiety because you know he is listening. You can also receive the assurance of God's love and concern for you through the promises he gives in his Word. Turn to him today to experience his loving care for you.

God's Companionship

You go before me and follow me. You place your hand of blessing on my head. . . . I can never escape from your Spirit! I can never get away from your presence!

PSALM 139:5, 7

The Bible promises that when you have a relationship with God, he is always with you. As you seek him through prayer, you start to see evidence of his presence with you. You notice his movement in your everyday life, recognize him leading you, and experience his love blessing you.

God's Glory

When the Great Shepherd appears, you will receive a crown of never-ending glory and honor. . . . In his kindness God called you to share in his eternal glory by means of Christ Jesus. So after you have suffered a little while, he will restore, support, and strengthen you, and he will place you on a firm foundation.

1 PETER 5:4, 10

In the midst of suffering, you may feel as though your pain will never end. But in comparison with eternity, your present suffering lasts only for "a little while." Be encouraged by the promises of God: He will restore what has been lost, support you with comfort and provision, strengthen you to overcome, and place you on the firm foundation of his unchanging love. And as a crowning gift, you will share in his glory forever!

God's Guidance

Trust in the LORD with all your heart; do not depend on your own understanding. Seek his will in all you do, and he will show you which path to take.

PROVERBS 3:5-6

In order to get good guidance, you have to know where to put your trust. People who are traveling in unfamiliar territory must rely on accurate maps and road signs to arrive at their intended destination. Someone who is critically ill must rely on a medical expert to prescribe the proper treatment. In the same way, you must realize your own spiritual limitations and rely on God's Word—the believer's instruction manual—in matters of faith. You will never understand all of life's complexities, but the Lord does. Trust him to guide you and show you the best way to go.

God's Love

God showed how much he loved us by sending his one and only Son into the world so that we might have eternal life through him. This is real love—not that we loved God, but that he loved us and sent his Son as a sacrifice to take away our sins.

1 JOHN 4:9-10

Real love is being willing to sacrifice much—even life itself—for the good of someone else. You know for certain how much God loves you because he allowed his Son to take the punishment for your sin by dying in your place to free you from eternal judgment. Think of it: God's Son died so that you could live forever with him. No wonder John wrote, "This is real love"!

God's Plan

We are God's masterpiece. He has created us anew in Christ Jesus, so we can do the good things he planned for us long ago.

EPHESIANS 2:10

Creativity is built into every human being. And because God created you, you are a product of his creativity! God wants you to use the unique gifts he fashioned in you to serve others. You can express your creativity and glorify him in countless ways—through worship and singing, through loving and helping others, through your trade or craft, and through analyzing and solving problems. As God's creation, you have a responsibility to reflect God's creative nature in appropriate ways that honor him and help fulfill his plan for your life.

God's Power

It is not by force nor by strength, but by my Spirit, says the LORD of Heaven's Armies.

ZECHARIAH 4:6

The Holy Spirit is the power of God that lives in every believer. When you yield control of your life to the Lord, he releases his power within you—power to resist temptation, to have wisdom in all circumstances, and to persevere in living for him here on Earth while clinging to the promise of eternal life in heaven. Through his Spirit, God will give you the power you need to do everything he asks.

God's Presence

Nothing can ever separate us from God's love. . . .
No power in the sky above or in the earth below—
indeed, nothing in all creation will ever be able to
separate us from the love of God that is revealed
in Christ Jesus our Lord.

ROMANS 8:38-39

Have you ever felt desperately alone and rejected? Perhaps a best friend deserted you or the marriage you hoped for never materialized or the person you married wants out. Maybe your child has turned against you or your parents and friends don't seem to care about your needs. God says, "Do not be afraid, for I am with you" (Isaiah 43:5). He promises to love you and stay with you no matter what. When you're hurting, let the peace of God's presence bring assurance that he will never separate himself from you.

God's Promises

Jesus Christ, the Son of God, does not waver between "Yes" and "No." . . . As God's ultimate "Yes," he always does what he says. For all of God's promises have been fulfilled in Christ with a resounding "Yes!" And through Christ, our "Amen" (which means "Yes") ascends to God for his glory.

2 CORINTHIANS 1:19-20

Jesus Christ is the Son of God, the Savior that God promised long ago. While on Earth, he was fully human and yet fully God. He lived a sinless life, then died on the cross to take the punishment for your sins. God resurrected him to prove his power over death and to assure you that if you believe in him as Lord, you also will be raised to eternal life. What rest we can take knowing that all of God's promises are met in our Savior.

God's Word

The grass withers and the flowers fade, but the word of our God stands forever.

ISAIAH 40:8

Almost everything on Earth experiences change—people, cultures, seasons. But the very Word of the almighty God never changes. Scripture is the only text that is "living." It is relevant for all people in all places and all times. It is as contemporary as the latest trend yet as lasting as eternity. The next time you feel unsteady from the world shifting around you, remember that the promises God makes in his Word—to love you, care for you, and be with you forever—will never change.

Grace

Sin is no longer your master, for you no longer live under the requirements of the law. Instead, you live under the freedom of God's grace.

ROMANS 6:14

Grace is undeserved favor. It is receiving mercy when you don't expect it or deserve it. The Bible says that God extends grace to you by offering you salvation—eternal life with him—when you believe and accept that Jesus, God's Son, died for your sins so you wouldn't have to pay that price. God's ultimate act of grace also gives you an example of how you are to extend grace to others. Show kindness by being quick to forgive and generous in love—even when others disappoint you or don't deserve it.

Grief

[Jesus said,] "God blesses those who mourn, for they will be comforted."

MATTHEW 5:4

Grief brings suffering, anxiety, confusion, restlessness, pain, heartache, and plenty of tears. Like a stabbing pain, it tortures your soul and robs you of the joy of living. But you can find comfort in knowing that Jesus extends the same care to you that he showed to many of his followers in the Bible. Rest assured that even when you go through dark times of grief, God is with you, blessing you and giving you hope.

Guidance

The LORD directs the steps of the godly. He delights in every detail of their lives. Though they stumble, they will never fall, for the LORD holds them by the hand.

PSALM 37:23-24

Don't let failure bring you down. Always get up and try again. Many inspiring success stories tell of people who failed numerous times but never gave up. Most importantly, never give up on your relationship with God. He promises to guide you through both your successes and your failures, walking with you each step of the way until you reach the ultimate success of eternal life with him.

Happiness

I know the LORD is always with me. . . . He is right beside me. No wonder my heart is glad, and I rejoice.

PSALM 16:8-9

Is happiness merely a fleeting emotion, or is it a permanent state of being? The Bible says it can be both. There is happiness that is a reaction to our surroundings, which is temporary; and there is happiness that is above and beyond everyday moments, which is strong and lasting. If temporary happiness is all we have, we must keep finding good things and experiences to keep us feeling that way. But those who have the joy that comes from God don't need experiences to keep them happy. They know that no matter what happens, God is with them and promises them lasting hope and happiness.

Healing

He personally carried our sins in his body on the cross so that we can be dead to sin and live for what is right. By his wounds you are healed.

1 PETER 2:24

A congenital disease is raging within you—it is called sin. Sin takes not only a physical, mental, and emotional toll on your well-being but a spiritual one as well. Thankfully, Jesus promises complete healing through the antidote of forgiveness. When you ask him to forgive you, a miraculous healing takes place, and sin no longer controls the way you live.

Heartbreak

The LORD is close to the brokenhearted;
he rescues those whose spirits are crushed.

PSALM 34:18

There is no quick cure for a broken heart. Taking a pill twice a day for two weeks will not treat it. A broken heart needs a different kind of healing. While others can help lessen your pain through generous doses of compassion, listening, love, comfort, encouragement, and blessing, God is the master healer. When you are hurting, move toward God. He promises to draw close to you and be your greatest source of comfort and healing.

Heart Change

I will give you a new heart, and I will put a new spirit in you. I will take out your stony, stubborn heart and give you a tender, responsive heart.

EZEKIEL 36:26

When you surrender control of your life to God, he gives you a new nature and a new desire to please him. He renews your heart as you humble yourself before him, turn away from past sinful habits, and make a daily effort to connect with him. And while you're doing these things, your love for him grows. God can change even the hardest heart into an obedient and loving heart. Are you willing to let him change you?

Heaven

I heard a loud shout from the throne, saying, "Look, God's home is now among his people! He will live with them, and they will be his people. God himself will be with them. He will wipe every tear from their eyes, and there will be no more death or sorrow or crying or pain. All these things are gone forever."

REVELATION 21:3-4

Scripture promises that one day God will create a new heaven and a new earth, where he will live among his people. Never again will anyone be tempted to sin or experience struggles or pain or death. Instead they will have everlasting joy. The best this world has to offer can't even begin to compare with the glory that is to come!

Help

He lifted me out of the pit of despair, out of the mud and the mire. He set my feet on solid ground and steadied me as I walked along.

PSALM 40:2

You need not pray for the Lord to be with you in times of crisis—he already is. God promises to carry you through your despair, give you firm footing on the other side, and walk with you in all the days to come.

Holiness

Our High Priest offered himself to God as a single sacrifice for sins, good for all time. Then he sat down in the place of honor at God's right hand. . . . By that one offering he forever made perfect those who are being made holy.

HEBREWS 10:12, 14

It is not possible to be holy on your own because you were born with a bent toward sin. But when you allow the Holy Spirit to control your mind and actions, you take the first important step toward becoming holy. Holiness here on earth does not equal being perfect; it means relying on the Holy Spirit to change you more and more into the likeness of Jesus. Yet God promises that one day you will at last be made perfect in heaven.

Holy

Even before he made the world, God loved us and chose us in Christ to be holy and without fault in his eyes.

EPHESIANS 1:4

God does not see you as holy because you are sinless but because his Son, Jesus, took away your sins when he died on the cross. Though as a believer you sincerely try to live in obedience to God's Word, the truth is that only Jesus lived a sinless life. And because of his sacrifice, God now sees you as holy. What amazing assurance! God sent his Son to die for your sins, and now you stand perfect before him.

Holy Spirit

[Jesus said,] "When the Father sends the Advocate as my representative—that is, the Holy Spirit—he will teach you everything and will remind you of everything I have told you."

JOHN 14:26

Jesus promised the gift of the Holy Spirit to his followers—an advocate who would always be with them after he rose from the dead and ascended into heaven. Now, anyone who believes in Jesus as their Savior has the Holy Spirit living inside of them. The Holy Spirit helps you understand the deep truths of God, convicts you of sin, teaches you how to live a life that pleases God, gives you words to pray, enables you to resist temptation, and assures you that you are a child of God. Thank God for giving you his Holy Spirit, and pray expectantly that he will release more and more of the Spirit's power in your life.

Home

[Jesus said,] *"There is more than enough room in my Father's home. If this were not so, would I have told you that I am going to prepare a place for you?"*

JOHN 14:2

When you travel, it's comforting to know you have a place to stay at the end of the day. You can have this same assurance for the end of your life. Not only is there a heaven, but Jesus is also making preparations for your arrival. Heaven is more than a paradise you will visit on vacation; it is an eternal home where you will live in joyful fellowship with your heavenly Father and your heavenly family. Though death is a great unknown, Jesus Christ has gone before you, and he is preparing a glorious place for you to stay. If you know and love Jesus, you can be confident that your room is ready and waiting.

Honesty

Who may climb the mountain of the LORD? Who may stand in his holy place? Only those whose hands and hearts are pure, who . . . never tell lies. They will receive the LORD's blessing and have a right relationship with God their savior.

PSALM 24:3-5

God requires honesty from you because honesty shows purity, integrity, and a desire to do what is true and right. Honesty creates trust, and trust is the basis of all relationships. You do not honor God if you cheat or take advantage of others to get ahead. He wants you to be completely honest—with him, yourself, and others. After all, when you are honest in even the smallest details, you gain some distinct advantages: a clear conscience, the trust and respect of others, and God's blessing.

Hope

We live with great expectation, and we have a priceless inheritance—an inheritance that is kept in heaven for you, pure and undefiled, beyond the reach of change and decay. And through your faith, God is protecting you by his power until you receive this salvation, which is ready to be revealed on the last day for all to see. So be truly glad. There is wonderful joy ahead, even though you must endure many trials for a little while.

1 PETER 1:3-6

We all have an expectation for good in our lives, even in the midst of adversity. At times we place our hope in things that fail us or don't last, but God gives us something to hope in that can never be taken away: the hope of heaven. Looking forward to eternal life with our Creator gives us confident joy in the face of uncertainty. As we meditate on the wonderful promise of eternity, it anchors our souls in the peace of knowing we have a future with him.

Identity

When you believed in Christ, he identified you as his own by giving you the Holy Spirit, whom he promised long ago. The Spirit is God's guarantee that he will give us the inheritance he promised and that he has purchased us to be his own people. He did this so we would praise and glorify him.

EPHESIANS 1:13-14

Finding your identity in Christ is the most important thing you can do during your time on Earth. When you believe in Jesus Christ, God gives you the Holy Spirit to prove that you belong to God and are guaranteed your inheritance of eternal life. When you are tempted to find your identity in other places, look to God's Word to show you who you really are—his very own child, known and loved by him.

Impossible Situations

Jesus looked at them intently and said, "Humanly speaking, it is impossible. But with God everything is possible."

MATTHEW 19:26

God specializes in doing the impossible. The end of your ability is the beginning of his. The God who spoke all creation into being can do the impossible for you. But you must believe that he can and that he wants to. When you try to cope with problems using your own strength, you easily become overwhelmed. But when you focus on God, you become aware of his power at work in your life. Then your impossibilities become God's opportunities.

Inheritance

Now you are no longer a slave but God's own child. And since you are his child, God has made you his heir.

GALATIANS 4:7

Belonging to God means you no longer stand guilty before him and are no longer a slave to your sinful nature. As God's child, you are forgiven and free to receive all the privileges of belonging to his family. Some of these privileges include complete acceptance by God, a clear sense of purpose, victory over sin, and the security of knowing you will live with God forever.

Intercession

The Holy Spirit helps us in our weakness. For example, we don't know what God wants us to pray for. But the Holy Spirit prays for us with groanings that cannot be expressed in words.

ROMANS 8:26

God gives you his Holy Spirit as your personal intercessor. When you don't know what to pray, the Holy Spirit will pray for you. God promises that you never have to worry about what to say to him. His Spirit will pray on your behalf even when you don't know how to express what kind of help you need.

Intimacy with God

Even when I walk through the darkest valley,
I will not be afraid, for you are close beside me.
Your rod and your staff protect and comfort me.

PSALM 23:4

Intimacy with God helps you see his personal touch in your life. He is your creator and shepherd. He wants to communicate with you, watch over you, care for you, advise you, and give you his joy and blessings. When you stay close to him, he will guide you step by step, bringing you comfort and protection along the way. Look for him in your life today, and you will see that he is right beside you.

Jesus

Mary responded, . . . "The Mighty One is holy, and he has done great things for me. He shows mercy from generation to generation to all who fear him. His mighty arm has done tremendous things!"

LUKE 1:46, 49-51

It may be hard to picture our mighty God, who created the heavens and the earth, sending his people a Savior in the form of a baby to redeem the world. But Jesus grew up with great trust in his Father and lived a sinless life, healing countless people, calming storms, and ultimately conquering the grave. He is mighty enough to conquer your troubles too. Jesus promises that through him you can have ultimate victory!

Joy

You will show me the way of life, granting me the joy of your presence and the pleasures of living with you forever.

PSALM 16:11

God does not promise that your life will always be happy. In fact, the Bible acknowledges that problems will come your way. But God does promise lasting joy for all who sincerely follow him. If you trust him, you have the assurance that the God of the universe loves you, wants to know you, promises to comfort and care for you, and has guaranteed an eternal future with him. This kind of joy stays with you despite your problems, and it helps you get through them without being overwhelmed.

Justification

We are made right with God by placing our faith in Jesus Christ. And this is true for everyone who believes, no matter who we are.

ROMANS 3:22

God's salvation is available to all people. It doesn't matter what sins you've committed in the past or who you are today. He loves everyone equally and wants them to be saved from eternal death. When you decide to follow Jesus Christ and ask him to forgive your sins, he makes you into a new creation. In his eyes, it's as though you had never sinned. You are clean and pure—justified and made right—just as he sees all who believe.

Kindness

The LORD is merciful and compassionate, slow to get angry and filled with unfailing love. . . . The LORD is righteous in everything he does; he is filled with kindness.

PSALM 145:8, 17

God didn't just create kindness; he *is* kindness. He promises to show mercy when you don't deserve it and to be patient when you're doing something wrong. In other words, he promises to love you unconditionally, even when you don't return his love. And if God is this kind to us, how can we not show the same kindness to others? The next time you find yourself struggling to be patient or loving toward others, remember how greatly God has shown his kindness to you.

Knowing Jesus

Christ is the visible image of the invisible God.
He existed before anything was created and
is supreme over all creation. . . . Christ is also
the head of the church, which is his body. He
is the beginning, supreme over all who rise from
the dead. So he is first in everything. For God
in all his fullness was pleased to live in Christ,
and through him God reconciled everything
to himself. He made peace with everything
in heaven and on earth by means of Christ's
blood on the cross.

COLOSSIANS 1:15, 18-20

These verses assure you that Jesus Christ is
in control of everything and that all things are
possible through him. The more you get to
know Jesus, the more you will see how he loves
and cares for you and the more confident you
will be that he keeps his promises.

Limitations

All glory to God, who is able, through his mighty power at work within us, to accomplish infinitely more than we might ask or think.

EPHESIANS 3:20

In God's unlimited knowledge and power, he created human beings with limitations. He did not do this to discourage his children but to help them realize their utter need for him. After all, it is in your weakness that God's strength shines the brightest. When you accomplish something beyond your normal abilities, you know that God is working through you. Jesus said, "What is impossible for people is possible with God" (Luke 18:27). The next time life makes you aware of your limitations, see it as an opportunity for God's power to overcome your human limitations. Eagerly anticipate how God will work through you to accomplish more than you could have ever dreamed.

Love

Love is patient and kind. Love is not jealous or boastful or proud or rude. It does not demand its own way. It is not irritable, and it keeps no record of being wronged. It does not rejoice about injustice but rejoices whenever the truth wins out. Love never gives up, never loses faith, is always hopeful, and endures through every circumstance.

1 CORINTHIANS 13:4-7

These well-known verses are some of the most eloquent and accurate descriptions of love ever written. Contrary to popular opinion, true love is first a courageous commitment and an unwavering choice to care for another person; only then does it produce powerful feelings. When you possess the qualities and practice the behaviors described in these verses, satisfaction and fulfillment will most certainly follow.

Loyalty

The LORD leads with unfailing love and faithfulness all who keep his covenant and obey his demands.

PSALM 25:10

Loyalty can be defined as a highly personal form of commitment. It says, "No matter what happens around us or between us, there is no fear, doubt, or hurt that could make me turn my back on you." When two people are loyal to each other, their relationship is secure and solid. But if one or both are disloyal, they live with insecurity and fear. The Bible teaches that loyalty is part of the very character of God. He expresses his loyalty by refusing to give up on you no matter how often you disappoint him with your sin. In turn, you express loyalty to God by obeying his Word and continually walking with him.

Mercy

His anger lasts only a moment, but his favor lasts a lifetime! Weeping may last through the night, but joy comes with the morning.

PSALM 30:5

One of the greatest misrepresentations some people make of God is that he is an angry old man. The Bible promises that God is kind and merciful and will always be ready to receive you with love when you confess your sin and seek a relationship with him. Instead of responding to his children with fierce anger and punishment, God corrects them with gentle discipline that is an expression of his love in action.

Mistakes

He has removed our sins as far from us as the east is from the west.

PSALM 103:12

There is a difference between making a mistake and committing a sin. For example, unintentionally hurting someone with your words is a mistake, while gossiping about or slandering someone is a sin. You can often avoid repeating a mistake by studying where you went wrong in the past or by thinking through your words and actions ahead of time. But to avoid repeating a sin, you need God's help. The regret you feel over your sin indicates that you want to change your ways. When you confess your sin to God, he promises to remove your guilt and help you do better next time.

Money

Don't love money; be satisfied with what you have. For God has said, "I will never fail you. I will never abandon you."

HEBREWS 13:5

You can experience true contentment only when you have a proper perspective of eternity. Your life should not be about how much you accumulate on Earth but how much you send on to heaven. Your heart and soul—what makes up who you are—follow you into eternity, while the money and possessions that make up what you have stay here.

Neediness

[Jesus said,] "God blesses those who are poor and realize their need for him, for the Kingdom of Heaven is theirs."

MATTHEW 5:3

If you believe Jesus died to take the punishment for your sins and recognize that only he can forgive you, the Bible promises that you will have eternal life. You cannot earn your way into heaven; it is God's gift to those who admit their need for Jesus.

New Beginnings

Great is his faithfulness; his mercies begin afresh each morning.

LAMENTATIONS 3:23

Life is a series of beginnings, and how you enter into them makes all the difference. Although the thought of starting fresh can sometimes make you anxious, remember that you experience new beginnings all the time. Each day brings new opportunities, including chances to get to know God better and to start over with a better attitude toward the circumstances and people in your life. God's mercy toward you is new every morning, no matter how you treated him or others just the day before. That means you don't have to be burdened by yesterday's failures or regrets but can look forward to a new beginning today.

New Life

Anyone who belongs to Christ has become a new person. The old life is gone; a new life has begun!

2 CORINTHIANS 5:17

Have you ever dreamed of a fresh start? One where you could leave behind past mistakes and regrets and start over again? Jesus promises that those who believe he is the Son of God will become new people. God literally changes them from the inside out. Their old life disappears, and a new one begins! Rejoice in the fact that God is delighted to give you new life.

Overcoming

[Jesus said,] "Here on earth you will have many trials and sorrows. But take heart, because I have overcome the world."

JOHN 16:33

Perhaps the best way God helps you deal with problems is by guaranteeing you a future time and place where there will be no problems. Here on Earth you may suffer from problems and worries because of sin. But no matter what your future holds, you can hold on to Jesus' promises that he has overcome this world and its troubles. You can be sure that heaven will be full of joy and free from pain and worries.

Peace

[Jesus said,] "I am leaving you with a gift—peace of mind and heart. And the peace I give is a gift the world cannot give. So don't be troubled or afraid."

JOHN 14:27

When you feel afraid, remember that no enemy or adversity can take away your most important blessings—your relationship with God, his forgiveness of your sins, and your eternal salvation. These remain secure even when your world falls apart, giving you great peace. Your situation may be genuinely threatening, but God has not abandoned you, and he promises to stay with you. Even if your troubles should end in death, God will usher you into his very presence.

Peacemaking

Wherever there is jealousy and selfish ambition, there you will find disorder and evil of every kind. . . . Those who are peacemakers will plant seeds of peace and reap a harvest of righteousness.

JAMES 3:16, 18

Peace and security come when you live in harmony with God's commands. God's two most important commands are to love him and to love others (see Matthew 22:36-40). When you put your own desires above the needs of others, turmoil and confusion can dominate your life. And when you follow your own rules instead of God's standards, chaos reigns. But when you allow God's commands to rule your life, order and purpose are restored. You grow in wisdom and find the peace your mind and heart desire.

Persecution

[Jesus said,] "God blesses you when people mock you and persecute you and lie about you and say all sorts of evil things against you because you are my followers."

MATTHEW 5:11

If you are ever persecuted for your faith, be encouraged by the fact that many other faithful believers have stood or are standing strong in the face of persecution. The Bible says that suffering for Jesus' sake is an honor. It is evidence of the depth of your love and commitment to him. Persecution also helps you know the heart of Jesus more deeply as you empathize with his sufferings and remember what he went through so you can live with him forever.

Perseverance

God, who began the good work within you, will continue his work until it is finally finished on the day when Christ Jesus returns. . . . Looking forward to what lies ahead, I press on to reach the end of the race and receive the heavenly prize for which God, through Christ Jesus, is calling us.

PHILIPPIANS 1:6; 3:13-14

To persevere is to endure with courage, even when the end is not in sight. Whatever you are facing, ask God to help you be faithful and do what is right, regardless of whether you see your desired results. Viewing your problems as opportunities to strengthen your faith and deepen your intimacy with Christ will grow your reliance on him, help you endure suffering, and give you the ability to persevere joyfully.

Persistence

[Jesus said,] "Keep on asking, and you will receive what you ask for. Keep on seeking, and you will find. Keep on knocking, and the door will be opened to you. For everyone who asks, receives. Everyone who seeks, finds. And to everyone who knocks, the door will be opened."

MATTHEW 7:7-8

There's more to prayer than just seeking an answer to a question or a solution to a problem. Whether or not you realize it, God often does more in your heart through your act of prayer than he does through his actual answer. As you continue coming to him with your praises and needs, taking the time to both talk to him and listen for his response, he promises that you will gain greater understanding of yourself, your situation, his purpose for you, and his direction for your life.

Perspective

We don't look at the troubles we can see now; rather, we fix our gaze on things that cannot be seen. For the things we see now will soon be gone, but the things we cannot see will last forever.

2 CORINTHIANS 4:18

God promises that the troubles looming in front of you today won't last forever. Your goal as a believer, then, is to turn your focus away from your trials and look instead to what will last— God's love, his gift of salvation, his care for you, and the promise of spending eternity in heaven with him. When you live with this perspective, you see your hurts and troubles as part of this temporary world and understand that the pain they bring won't continue forever. You can then have greater hope and confidence in God's promise of a new earth, where hurt and pain will no longer exist.

Pleasing God

Anyone who does what pleases God will live forever.

1 JOHN 2:17

When you obey God, you not only please him but are also able to enjoy life the way he meant for it to be enjoyed. Your relationships are more fulfilling, your life is full of integrity, and your conscience is clear. Most important, you will be able to one day enjoy life with God in a perfect world for all eternity.

Power

He gives power to the weak and strength to the powerless. Even youths will become weak and tired, and young men will fall in exhaustion. But those who trust in the LORD will find new strength. They will soar high on wings like eagles. They will run and not grow weary. They will walk and not faint.

ISAIAH 40:29-31

The more you recognize your own weaknesses and limitations, the more you will understand God's power at work within you. Strength can make you proud and self-sufficient, keeping you from praising God or turning to him for help. That is why God often works through your weaknesses and weariness, so long as you let him. Then there is no doubt that it is by *his* power—not your own—that you've been able to accomplish all that you have.

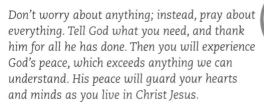

Prayer

Don't worry about anything; instead, pray about everything. Tell God what you need, and thank him for all he has done. Then you will experience God's peace, which exceeds anything we can understand. His peace will guard your hearts and minds as you live in Christ Jesus.

PHILIPPIANS 4:6-7

Don't ever be afraid to talk to God. When you get to know him, you'll discover that he's not a harsh dictator ready to punish you for every fault. Instead, you will see that he's a loving Father who wants to comfort, help, forgive, and bless you. The assurance of God's love gives you courage to come to him with any problem, struggle, or concern you might have. He promises to always listen, so approach him freely with your praises, joys, worries, and troubles.

Promises

God has given both his promise and his oath. These two things are unchangeable because it is impossible for God to lie. Therefore, we who have fled to him for refuge can have great confidence as we hold to the hope that lies before us.

HEBREWS 6:18

A wedding is one of the most sacred of ceremonies. The vows that a husband and wife take as they enter into marriage are full of beauty and boldness, intended to bind the two as long as they both shall live. Yet divorce statistics prove that even this sacred promise is not always taken seriously today. The opposite is true with God. His promises are anchored in his unchanging character and his steadfast love. He has never once broken a promise or told a lie. We can find great hope in his faithfulness and commitment to us.

Protection

My help comes from the LORD, who made heaven and earth! He will not let you stumble; the one who watches over you will not slumber. Indeed, he who watches over Israel never slumbers or sleeps. The LORD himself watches over you! The LORD stands beside you as your protective shade. . . . The LORD keeps watch over you as you come and go, both now and forever.

PSALM 121:2-5, 8

God promises to protect those who love him. But the ultimate fulfillment of this promise comes as God safeguards your soul so that you may live forever with him in heaven. Loving God and committing yourself to obeying him ensure that your soul will be in the right place for eternity. You can rest in this promise of his protection over you for all your days.

Provision

[Jesus said,] *"Your heavenly Father already knows all your needs. Seek the Kingdom of God above all else, and live righteously, and he will give you everything you need."*

MATTHEW 6:32-33

The Bible promises that God will supply all your needs. However, disappointment or problems can arise when your definition of your needs is different from his. Rather than letting your own desires hinder your relationship with him, study God's Word to discover what he says you really need for a fulfilling life.

Purpose

I cry out to God Most High, to God who will fulfill his purpose for me.

PSALM 57:2

God has both a general purpose and a specific purpose for your life. In a general sense, you have been chosen by God to let the love of Jesus shine through you to make an impact on others. More specifically, God has given you unique spiritual gifts and wants you to use them to make a worthwhile contribution within your sphere of influence. The more you fulfill God's general purpose for you, the clearer your specific purpose will become.

Reconciliation with God

Since we have been made right in God's sight by the blood of Christ, he will certainly save us from God's condemnation. For since our friendship with God was restored by the death of his Son while we were still his enemies, we will certainly be saved through the life of his Son.

ROMANS 5:9-10

Because we often like to be in control of our own lives, one of the hardest things to accept is that we don't make up the rules—God does. God says that sin deserves eternal death, and every one of us except Jesus has sinned. Your assurance for salvation is based on the fact that Jesus stood in your place and took the judgment you deserved for your sin. Because of Jesus' sacrifice, God promises that he no longer considers you an enemy but a friend—even his own child. What a comfort to know that you have been reconciled with God.

Regret

He saved us, not because of the righteous things we had done, but because of his mercy. He washed away our sins, giving us a new birth and new life through the Holy Spirit.

TITUS 3:5

Your regrets are like a dirty window, preventing you from seeing clearly what is in front of you. They cloud your vision and disturb your thoughts. But God is in the cleaning business. He washes away not only the sins of your past but also the guilt you still feel over them. If God can completely forget your sins, so can you. You can thank him for washing you clean and choose to move forward joyfully, leaving behind the burden of regret.

Rejoicing

Even though the fig trees have no blossoms, and there are no grapes on the vines; even though the olive crop fails, and the fields lie empty and barren; even though the flocks die in the fields, and the cattle barns are empty, yet I will rejoice in the Lord! I will be joyful in the God of my salvation! The Sovereign Lord is my strength!

HABAKKUK 3:17-19

The more you despair during hard times, the more those times will drag you down. But the more you reach out to God with hope and gratitude, recognizing that your circumstances are temporary, the more your perspective and attitude will change for the good. No matter what you are going through, you can respond joyfully to the God who offers you peace and strength to calm your heart and mind.

Relationship with God

*The LORD says, "I will rescue those who love me.
I will protect those who trust in my name. When
they call on me, I will answer; I will be with them
in trouble. I will rescue and honor them. I will
reward them with a long life and give them my
salvation."*

PSALM 91:14-16

God loves you because he made you. You are
not a random by-product of evolution but
rather a child of God. He created you in his
own image so you could have a relationship
with him. God desires your love and friendship,
and he is pursuing you now. When you allow
God access to your heart and know his in
return, you discover the purpose for which
he made you.

Reputation

Never let loyalty and kindness leave you! Tie them around your neck as a reminder. Write them deep within your heart. Then you will find favor with both God and people, and you will earn a good reputation.

PROVERBS 3:3-4

Everyone has a reputation. Whether you intentionally try to project a certain image or couldn't care less what others think, people still form an opinion of you based on your personality, character, behavior, and abilities. A good reputation can help you make friends and gain respect, while a bad reputation can attract others of ill repute or leave you feeling isolated, shunned, and disrespected. But God promises you will earn a good reputation when you show his kindness, loyalty, and love to your neighbors.

Resisting Temptation

Humble yourselves before God. Resist the devil, and he will flee from you.

JAMES 4:7

When you believe and live out the truths taught in God's Word, you have an upper hand in the battle against evil. If you humble yourself before God and ask him for help, he will give you discernment and protection against Satan and his demons, who continually fight for your soul. The Word of God and the Holy Spirit are powerful resources you can always turn to for help in resisting your enemy. Stand strong and confident in your faith, and you can be sure that God will help you fight your battles and make you victorious.

Responsibility

[Jesus said,] *"To those who use well what they are given, even more will be given, and they will have an abundance. But from those who do nothing, even what little they have will be taken away."*

MATTHEW 25:29

It seems more and more that people avoid taking responsibility for their actions; nothing is ever anyone's fault. But God promises that if you take responsibility for your actions and use well the gifts he has given you, he will give you more opportunities and more blessings. In the end, each person will be responsible for his or her own decisions, behavior, and relationships. Show responsibility in how you use the gifts and opportunities God has given you, and he will reward you.

Rest

Jesus said, "Come to me, all of you who are weary and carry heavy burdens, and I will give you rest. Take my yoke upon you. Let me teach you, because I am humble and gentle at heart, and you will find rest for your souls. For my yoke is easy to bear, and the burden I give you is light."

MATTHEW 11:28-30

When you visit family or friends who live far away and spend the night with them, usually they've prepared a room for you to make you comfortable and help you rest. What comfort it is to know that God does the same. When you come to him, he prepares a place where you can feel safe and rest quietly. In his presence, the burdens of the world are put into perspective, and you can find the spiritual refreshment you crave. Go to the Creator of rest and linger with him. Only he can give you true rest.

Restoration

The Lord nurses them when they are sick and restores them to health.

PSALM 41:3

God can heal any pain—a broken body and a broken heart. As you wait for God's healing, don't give up. Believe that he can and will fully restore you—however he chooses to do so. Until then, allow him to comfort you and give you the strength you need to keep going.

Resurrection

Jesus told her, "I am the resurrection and the life. Anyone who believes in me will live, even after dying."

JOHN 11:25

Jesus' resurrection is key to the Christian faith. In John 2:19, Jesus said, "Destroy this temple, and in three days I will raise it up." Just as he promised, Jesus rose from the dead. You can be confident, then, that God will keep his other promises too. And as a believer, you can be certain of your own resurrection since Jesus has power over death. The resurrection of Jesus proves that he is more than just a leader or prophet. He is the Son of God, and he brings eternal life to all who believe in him.

Revival

The instructions of the LORD are perfect, reviving the soul. The decrees of the LORD are trustworthy, making wise the simple.

PSALM 19:7

Reading and meditating on God's Word revives your soul. His words are living and therefore relevant to your current situation, no matter what it may be. The almighty God speaks to you through the Bible, and his words bring peace, strength, comfort, wisdom, and hope—the very nourishment you need for revival. Sin starves your soul, but God's Word revives it.

Rewards

No eye has seen, no ear has heard, and no mind has imagined what God has prepared for those who love him.

1 CORINTHIANS 2:9

Nonbelievers might ask, "If Christians suffer like everybody else, why bother living for God and following him?" A "why bother" attitude might be understandable if rewards and pleasure were all that Christians sought. But this perspective ignores two vital reasons for our faith: First, when we obey God, our relationships are fulfilling, our lives display integrity, and our consciences are clear. Second, this life is not all there is. The Bible clearly says in John 3:16 that those who trust Jesus Christ for the forgiveness of their sins receive the promise of eternal life. Your faithfulness may or may not result in earthly riches or gain, but your rewards in heaven will be greater than you can imagine.

Salvation

The wages of sin is death, but the free gift of God is eternal life through Christ Jesus our Lord.

ROMANS 6:23

God promises the gift of salvation to everyone who accepts it. When you confess your sins, ask for forgiveness and believe that because Jesus died for your sins, you are saved from the punishment you deserve. God looks at you as though you had never sinned and promises you eternal life in heaven.

Satisfaction

[Jesus said,] "Those who drink the water I give will never be thirsty again. It becomes a fresh, bubbling spring within them, giving them eternal life."

JOHN 4:14

At some point all people search for something to quench their thirsting souls. But too many try filling their lives with the wrong things. The key to being truly satisfied is to fill yourself with something that will last. God promises that when you drink from the water he gives through his Word and Spirit, you will be fulfilled and satisfied for all eternity.

Scripture

All Scripture is inspired by God and is useful to teach us what is true and to make us realize what is wrong in our lives. It corrects us when we are wrong and teaches us to do what is right. God uses it to prepare and equip his people to do every good work.

2 TIMOTHY 3:16-17

If you buy a new computer but neglect to read the instruction manual, you'll miss out on many of its features. You'll be operating with just enough knowledge to perform basic functions. The same is true of reading the Bible. Most of us read just enough to get by and miss much of what God's Word has to offer. Read the Bible daily so you can thoroughly understand everything God wants you to know. Then you will be able to live at peak performance.

Searching

From there you will search again for the Lord your God. And if you search for him with all your heart and soul, you will find him.

DEUTERONOMY 4:29

God wants everyone to know him and reveals himself to all who seek him. Yet sometimes you may find yourself wanting to hide from God. You may blame him when your relationship feels distant or claim that he is the one who has turned a blind eye. But perhaps during those times you're actually hiding from God because finding him means your life will change radically. God is always trying to show himself to you; the question is, Do you really want to find him? He promises to be found when you seek him wholeheartedly.

Second Coming

[Jesus said,] "At last, the sign that the Son of Man is coming will appear in the heavens, and there will be deep mourning among all the peoples of the earth. And they will see the Son of Man coming on the clouds of heaven with power and great glory. And he will send out his angels with the mighty blast of a trumpet, and they will gather his chosen ones from all over the world—from the farthest ends of the earth and heaven."

MATTHEW 24:30-31

One of the greatest promises in the Bible is that Jesus will come again. He will come to judge the wicked and bring justice for their wrongs. And he will come to rescue all who believe in him as Lord. We will be gathered together to live with him forever.

Security

[Jesus said,] "Don't be afraid of those who want to kill your body; they cannot touch your soul. Fear only God, who can destroy both soul and body in hell."

MATTHEW 10:28

Although God often protects his people from physical harm, he is more concerned about protecting their souls from eternal harm. When you commit to following his ways, he commits to bringing you safely into eternity with him. So ask God for his protection. He is strong when you are weak. He is your safe haven when you are vulnerable and under attack. As his child, you have the power and presence of God protecting you.

Seeking Approval

The Kingdom of God is not a matter of what we eat or drink, but of living a life of goodness and peace and joy in the Holy Spirit. If you serve Christ with this attitude, you will please God, and others will approve of you, too.

ROMANS 14:17-18

In all you do, seek God's approval first. Sometimes doing what pleases God pleases others, especially godly people, but God has many enemies who love evil and may reject your words and deeds. Still your ultimate purpose is to please the God who made you and redeemed you, no matter what others may think. Focus on him; he promises you will always receive his approval.

Self-Control

Let the Holy Spirit guide your lives. Then you won't be doing what your sinful nature craves. . . . Those who belong to Christ Jesus have nailed the passions and desires of their sinful nature to his cross and crucified them there.

GALATIANS 5:16, 24

Because you were born with a sinful nature, you will always struggle to do what is right. But God understands your weaknesses, and he promises that the Holy Spirit will help you develop the desire to please him. As the Spirit leads you to obey God, you will develop more self-control and greater strength to fight and win the battle against your sinful nature.

Serving

We are many parts of one body, and we all belong to each other. In his grace, God has given us different gifts for doing certain things well.

ROMANS 12:5-6

Just as all kinds of musical instruments are necessary to make up an orchestra, so all kinds of gifts and perspectives are needed to make up the church. In fact, God promises that he has given you a unique gift so that you can contribute well in the work of his Kingdom. And just as each unique instrument in an orchestra works together with the other instruments to make beautiful music, God often puts people with different gifts together so that their gifts may complement each other. It is through this diversity that the most progress in serving him and others can be made.

Showing God's Love

You are a chosen people. You are royal priests, a holy nation, God's very own possession. As a result, you can show others the goodness of God, for he called you out of the darkness into his wonderful light.

1 PETER 2:9

Have you ever searched through drawers and closets for a flashlight, only to discover once you found one that its batteries were dead? Although the flashlight had the potential to provide light, without new batteries it was useless. Like every believer, you have the light of Christ within you and therefore the potential to shine upon others and draw them to God. God promises that you will do amazing things if only you let him work through you.

Significance

[Jesus said,] "What is the price of two sparrows—one copper coin? But not a single sparrow can fall to the ground without your Father knowing it. . . . So don't be afraid; you are more valuable to God than a whole flock of sparrows."

MATTHEW 10:29, 31

Deep within every human heart lies a hunger for significance. We want our lives to count, to make a difference, to be worth something. Yet many people carry deep feelings of insignificance. Their lives are dominated not by their abilities but by their inabilities. Everywhere they look they see others who appear more successful or gifted. The Bible, however, says that every person has great value. You are significant not because of anything you can accomplish on your own, but because God loves you and promises that you are valuable to him.

Sin

Everyone has sinned; we all fall short of God's glorious standard. . . . If you openly declare that Jesus is Lord and believe in your heart that God raised him from the dead, you will be saved.

ROMANS 3:23; 10:9

God loves all people, but he brings eternal salvation only to those who confess their sin and believe in him. Understanding this difference is a matter of life and death. God loves you unconditionally, but he does not approve of sinful behavior. Sin separates you from God, but Jesus died and was resurrected to take away your sin and restore you to him. Knowing this is critical, for it is only then that you will realize how much God values you. When you confess your sins to him, seek his forgiveness, and commit to following Jesus, you will receive salvation in this life and the promise of eternal life in heaven.

Sorrow

You keep track of all my sorrows. You have collected all my tears in your bottle. You have recorded each one in your book.

PSALM 56:8

Even people who have a relationship with God through Jesus Christ grieve during times of loss. But Christians can grieve with hope. You may grieve because you have experienced the real pain of loss, but you can grieve with hope because you know that God notices your sorrow and will redeem your tragedy. God does not waste your sorrows but promises to bring good out of them when you let him do his transforming work in you.

Sovereignty

We know that God causes everything to work together for the good of those who love God and are called according to his purpose for them.

ROMANS 8:28

We can know God is sovereign because he is all-knowing, purposeful in everything he does, and always in control. These truths should impact the way we live by teaching us to rest in him. When we truly believe that God is in control of our circumstances and working everything together for our good, we acknowledge his power and sovereignty, giving him the glory and praise he deserves.

Spiritual Gifts

There are different kinds of spiritual gifts, but the same Spirit is the source of them all. There are different kinds of service, but we serve the same Lord. God works in different ways, but it is the same God who does the work in all of us.

1 CORINTHIANS 12:4-6

The abilities you have are gifts from God, and they are often clues that point to how God wants you to spend your time. Would God give you certain talents and spiritual gifts and then not ask you to use them? Perhaps you have a gift of faith, discernment, or encouragement that is clearly inspired by the Holy Spirit's presence within you. You may also have a natural inclination toward cooking, entertaining, managing a business, teaching, handling money, playing an instrument, or any number of other things. Use the gifts you have to bring honor and glory to God. Then you will be right where you need to be to discover God's will and to accomplish his purpose for you.

Spiritual Maturity

Let your roots grow down into him, and let your lives be built on him. Then your faith will grow strong in the truth you were taught, and you will overflow with thankfulness.

COLOSSIANS 2:7

Spiritual growth is like physical growth—you start very small and grow one day at a time. To mature, however, you need nourishment. As a believer, you're fed by challenging your mind in the study of God's Word—asking questions about it and seeking answers through prayer and the counsel of other believers. Do not be discouraged when you aren't growing as quickly as you would like. Instead, look at each day as a stepping-stone to reaching spiritual maturity.

Spiritual Nourishment

Jesus replied, "I am the bread of life. Whoever comes to me will never be hungry again. Whoever believes in me will never be thirsty."

JOHN 6:35

Jesus is the spiritual nourishment your soul craves. His daily presence satisfies your deepest hunger. He meets your needs, works good into your life, offers you peace of mind, and promises the gift of everlasting life. Feed your soul with Jesus, and you will be satisfied for eternity.

Steadfastness

Blessed are those who trust in the LORD and have made the LORD their hope and confidence. They are like trees planted along a riverbank, with roots that reach deep into the water. Such trees are not bothered by the heat or worried by long months of drought. Their leaves stay green, and they never stop producing fruit.

JEREMIAH 17:7-8

God uses your circumstances to help you and others grow. It's easy to be joyful and faithful when life is going well, but when life gets tough, believers have a unique opportunity to show how a relationship with God brings comfort, confidence, and hope. When you glorify God in the most difficult of circumstances, two wonderful things happen: You learn to rely on God instead of yourself, and others are blessed by seeing your faith and hope in action.

Strength

Don't be afraid, for I am with you. Don't be discouraged, for I am your God. I will strengthen you and help you. I will hold you up with my victorious right hand.

ISAIAH 41:10

It's easy to become overwhelmed by the challenges and struggles you face each day. But when you begin to see the obstacles in your life as opportunities for God to show you his strength, they will not seem so daunting. The hardships that frighten you may be the tools God is using to make you stronger and to equip you to fight life's battles. Come to God in prayer and allow him to work in your situation and give you his strength.

Suffering

We believers also groan, . . . for we long for our bodies to be released from sin and suffering. We, too, wait with eager hope for the day when God will give us our full rights as his adopted children, including the new bodies he has promised us.

ROMANS 8:23

God does not promise believers a life free from pain and suffering. If Christians didn't experience difficulty, others might see God only as some sort of magician who takes away the bad things in life. But when you have a relationship with God, he helps you, comforts you, and sometimes miraculously heals you. Most important, God will one day take away all your pain. Whatever you are experiencing is only temporary. You can be certain there is no hurt in heaven.

Temptation

God blesses those who patiently endure testing and temptation. Afterward they will receive the crown of life that God has promised to those who love him.

JAMES 1:12

Although God sometimes delivers you from difficult circumstances, he often calls you to an enduring faithfulness in the midst of temptations and trials. Endurance involves not only experiencing situations of suffering but also overcoming them with patience, hope, and joy. When you persevere and look to God for help in your temptations, he promises to reward you.

Testing

This High Priest of ours understands our weaknesses, for he faced all of the same testings we do, yet he did not sin. So let us come boldly to the throne of our gracious God. There we will receive his mercy, and we will find grace to help us when we need it most.

HEBREWS 4:15-16

In this life, we will face many situations where our faith will be tested. But how wonderful is it that Christ can empathize with our weaknesses since he, too, was tested during his time on earth? God uses testing to purify us and move us into spiritual maturity. As we overcome these trials, we will find ourselves with a more committed faith, deeper wisdom, and a more intimate relationship with God.

Thankfulness

Giving thanks is a sacrifice that truly honors me. If you keep to my path, I will reveal to you the salvation of God.

PSALM 50:23

The Bible says that thanking God is a sacrifice that honors him. It recognizes his work, mercy, provision, and blessing in your life. A thankful heart gives you a positive attitude and keeps you focused on all that God is doing for you rather than on the things you think you lack. Give thanks to God every day, for he promises to bless you with his salvation.

Thoughts

You will keep in perfect peace all who trust in you, all whose thoughts are fixed on you!

ISAIAH 26:3

There are many ways to achieve peace—or the semblance of peace—but genuine peace is found only by focusing your thoughts on God and developing a trusting relationship with him. Peace is not the absence of conflict but the presence of God. You receive peace of mind as the Holy Spirit guides you into God's purposes for your life and gives you an eternal perspective. You receive peace of heart as the Holy Spirit empowers you to live productively and comforts you in times of trouble.

Transformation

Let me reveal to you a wonderful secret. We will not all die, but we will all be transformed! It will happen in a moment, in the blink of an eye, when the last trumpet is blown. For when the trumpet sounds, those who have died will be raised to live forever. And we who are living will also be transformed. For our dying bodies must be transformed into bodies that will never die; our mortal bodies must be transformed into immortal bodies.

1 CORINTHIANS 15:51-53

One day you will be like Jesus. You will not be equal to him in power and authority, but you will resemble him in character and perfection. Your body will be transformed into an immortal body where sin can no longer harm you, and you will never again experience pain or sorrow.

Truth

Jesus told him, "I am the way, the truth, and the life. No one can come to the Father except through me."

JOHN 14:6

Jesus is the only way to heaven—that's the truth. You may want to buy your way in, work your way in, or think your way in, but the Bible is clear—Jesus Christ provides the only way to the place for which our souls long. Gratefully accepting this truth by believing in him and following him will put you on the path to life's most important destination.

Unchanging

Whatever is good and perfect is a gift coming down to us from God our Father, who created all the lights in the heavens. He never changes or casts a shifting shadow.

JAMES 1:17

What great comfort we can take in knowing that the character of God never changes. He is always reliable. No matter how the seasons in your life may change, and no matter what new situations you may face, God is with you. You can always count on his unchanging promises to help you and guide you.

Victory

LORD, I have so many enemies; so many are against me. . . . But you, O LORD, are a shield around me; you are my glory, the one who holds my head high. . . . Victory comes from you, O LORD.

PSALM 3:1, 3, 8

Evil can't stand the sight of Jesus. It can't bear to hear his name. So if your life clearly reflects the peace and light of Jesus, there is good news and bad news. The bad news is that you may face opposition and even persecution for your faith. Because Satan opposes Jesus, Satan is your enemy too. The good news is that even if the whole world is against you, God is for you. He promises to give you spiritual victories in this life and ultimate victory in heaven for eternity.

Weakness

Each time [God] said, "My grace is all you need. My power works best in weakness." So now I am glad to boast about my weaknesses, so that the power of Christ can work through me.

2 CORINTHIANS 12:9

One thing is certain: Everyone has weaknesses, so we must learn to live with failure. Strong character depends not on how often we fail but on how we respond to failure. Adam and Eve, for example, responded to failure by placing the blame on someone else rather than admitting their mistakes and seeking forgiveness. The apostle Paul, however, learned to appreciate his weaknesses and failures because God was working through them. Those who admit their failures and learn from them will go on to accomplish great things.

Wisdom

If you need wisdom, ask our generous God, and he will give it to you. He will not rebuke you for asking.

JAMES 1:5

When you are faced with a decision, you may be afraid to bring it before God because you think he has larger issues to deal with. But that is not the case. God loves you and wants to help you. He cares about your little decisions as much as your big ones. When you open the lines of communication with God, he releases his wisdom and resources to you.

SCRIPTURE INDEX